THOMPSON

SUBMACHINE GUN

CLASSIC WEAPONS SERIES

THOMPSON

SUBMACHINE GUN

CHRIS ELLIS

This edition first published in 1998 by
PRC Publishing Ltd,
Kiln House, 210 New Kings Road, London SW6 4NZ

This edition was produced in 1998 for the
Military Book Club in New York

Printed and bound in China

Acknowledgements
A big thank-you for the help of George Forty and Peter Chamberlain
in researching the photographs.

Contents

PAGE 2: A US Marine using the M28A1.

BELOW: American soldier at Altenberg, carrying his Thompson M1A1.

Introduction

Time 1.15pm, date 20 September 1926—it's a quiet lunchtime in a wide main street and people are still eating in the restaurants that flank it. Suddenly a big black limousine comes down the street clanging its gong like a police car. As it draws level with the biggest and grandest restaurant, a dark gun muzzle projects from a rear window of the car and there is a sudden clatter of what sounds like machine gun fire. People instinctively duck or dive for cover, but nothing happens. No ricochets, no broken glass, no injuries. The gun was firing blanks.

Inquisitive and startled bystanders look up puzzled, but the intended victim of the attack is restrained by a streetwise bodyguard, who instinctively realises that this is a decoy attack intended to attract attention and bring people out on to the street. The bodyguard is right: moments later a convoy of ten more closely spaced cars—ordinary looking sedans—come down the same street in the same direction, from the west. As they come abreast of the block containing the restaurant, muzzles project from the rear side windows of all the cars and machine gun fire erupts in mighty roar with bullets spraying the buildings flanking the restaurant. By the restaurant the cars stop and the guns concentrate fire on the restaurant itself. All windows shatter, doors cave in, and bits of wood and masonry fly everywhere. From the ninth car a man in overalls steps out, carrying an elegant gun with a big circular magazine. He kneels in the doorway of the restaurant and empties the 100-round magazine into the interior, sweeping the crockery from the tables and destroying most of the contents. While he does this, men with shotguns from the tenth car protect the convoy from approach at the rear. This final fusillade takes about ten seconds; the firing before that perhaps another twenty seconds. As the gunner runs out of ammunition, the lead car toots its horn three times, the men from the last two cars jump back in, and the entire ten-car convoy speeds off to the east.

No, this is not fiction. It is a description of a well-planned operation that used a new and formidable weapon to its best advantage, made enormous headlines at the time and was a massive embarrassment for the authorities. For this was not a spectacular military operation in some far flung enemy city: it took place in the heartland of the United States of America, in the town of Cicero, just two blocks from the city limits of the 'second city', Chicago.

At the time it was the most effective demonstration of the firepower of the Thompson SMG that the world had yet seen. The intended target of this ferocious attack was Chicago gang leader Al Capone, who was having lunch in the big restaurant, the Hawthorne, which he owned. Capone, well guarded, was eating at the back of the restaurant, with his back to the wall, the place to be if you had to be wary of attack. At this period, the latter half of the 1920s, gangland warfare was at its height in Chicago (and to a lesser extent in other American big cities), as rival big shots carved out and fought for territorial control of illicit drink supply. This was the period of Prohibition, and with it came Speakeasies, illicit stills and breweries, convoys of trucks carrying contraband by night, protection rackets, and the police and political corruption associated with the time. Huge tax-free profits could be made by the most ruthless and cleverest racketeers, and Capone became the dominant operator in the business, though in the late 1920s he had a lot of rivals eager to wipe him out.

Gangland killings were happening almost daily and had become so common-

place they were hardly reported any more. But until the latter part of 1925 gangsters had mainly used revolvers or shotguns—specially shotguns—as weapons. But these were not always efficient unless the victim could be trapped in his car or an enclosed space like a hotel lobby. So many intended assassinations ended up as woundings, from which the victim recovered and retaliated. Very few gang members were competent gunmen, hence the use of shotguns.

It was a 'minder' named Frank McErlane, once called 'the most brutal gunman who ever pulled a trigger in Chicago', who changed things. He hit upon the idea of acquiring a then little-considered weapon called the Thompson Submachine Gun. It was available commercially for as little as $175 because in the years of peace the military did not want it, and it had received scant publicity. On 25 September 1925 all that changed when McErlane used his newly acquired Thompson—unsuccessfully—in an attempt to eliminate a South Side gang leader, Spike O'Donnell. McErlane reasoned that the Thompson SMG was a much more efficient weapon than a shotgun for an assured killing, even though he missed his first victim who was quick witted enough to duck.

The Thompson SMG was so little known that the Chicago police who investigated the shooting were baffled at first, wondering how such a neat line of bullet holes could have been fired into a shop front. Somebody speculated that it might have been a volley from a row of marksmen, though the consensus was that it came from 'some sort of machine rifle'. By the time McErlane used the gun again, to blast a rival club two weeks later, the weapon had been identified by police and rival gangsters alike and from then on the 'Tommy Gun', also soon known as a 'Chicago Piano' or 'Chicago Violin'—a violin case was a favourite way to carry it — became the favoured hit weapon of gangland.

Al Capone was the next customer and his organisation acquired three very quickly. It was a handy weapon for a gangster, being under 3ft (90cm) in length, weighing about 20lb (9.1kg) with a 100-round magazine and under 9lb (4.1kg) without it, and above all being able to fire an endless stream of heavy .45in (11mm) bullets with great precision but requiring no great finesse on the part of the firer. The mayhem it caused prevented retaliation from those not similarly armed, and at close range it

ABOVE: 'On the side of Law and Order'. This slogan, with this picture, was used on much Auto-Ordnance Corporation sales literature in the 1920s. It shows an American policeman with a Model 1921A Thompson, fitted with 50-round Type L drum magazine.

ed one to every squad car. But the mayhem continued, and other cities such as Philadelphia and New York were blighted by gang fights with Tommy Guns, though never on the scale of Chicago. The most notorious happening of all was still to come, the St Valentine's Day Massacre of 14 February 1929, when Capone men, disguised as police and in a car marked as a police car, raided a North Side gang garage, lined up the occupants and mowed then down with Thompson SMGs. The outcry was enormous and public revulsion reached new heights. No subsequent gangland outrage ever came near it, and by 1933 Prohibition was at an end and there was much less reason for gangsters to fight.

Symbol of an era

But the Tommy Gun has remained an enduring symbol of that bloody era, immortalised in almost every Hollywood gangster film since, and it remains the most widely known hand gun. Strange to say, the gangland use of Thompson SMGs achieved a notoriety for the weapon out of all proportion to the number of guns used, for—as so often in criminal activities—the same few guns were passed around and used in numerous different incidents, as ballistics investigations often showed.

They also brought much needed publicity, but of quite the wrong kind, for the makers of the gun, the Auto-Ordnance Corporation of New York. The Tommy Gun became known as the 'gangster' gun, and this also affected the military attitude to it; the company was derided as the purveyor of weapons to gangland, despite the fact that it had no legal control on who bought the guns, as most sales were through local gun shops.

However, it was not much long after the St Valentine's Day Massacre, the company went into new management and there was a harder look at sales policy. In October 1930 it was announced that the company had suspended all sales 'other than for military purposes'. This not only eliminated sales to gangsters but it put out of the market all the civilian, prison and police

could do a lot of damage to both men and material. It could be legally purchased by anyone, too, at that time.

The Tommy Gun—'Lawn Mower' was another early nickname—changed the nature of gang warfare in 1926. Spectacular shootings and shoot-ups became more common, with the attack on Capone's HQ in Cicero the most blatant of all. The Tommy Gun really came to public attention in April 1926 when William McSwiggin, an up-and-coming young Assistant States Attorney in Chicago—and prosecutor of gangsters—was found shot down and dumped, victim of the vicious new weapon. On 11 October 1926, as he alighted from a car outside his HQ North Side gang leader Hymie Weiss was killed in the crossfire from Capone men with Thompson SMGs holed up in rooming houses. This was in broad daylight in the centre of Chicago. Not surprisingly, in the face of much firepower in January 1927 the Chicago Police Department ordered Thompson SMGs, 35 of them, and allocat-

the Valentine MASSACRE

authorities who had actually been much bigger purchasers of Thompson SMGs than anyone else. By that time the Thompson SMG was much in use with police and sheriff departments across the United States as well as by prison guards, bank guards and security men. The only concession made was that spare parts would be sold for existing guns. As military sales had been minimal up to that time, this had a devastating affect on the company's finances leading to changes of stockholders and ownership during the 1930s, and much writing-off of debt.

Gang warfare with Tommy Guns was not the first blow to the reputation of the Auto-Ordnance Corporation: in 1921 there had been a mighty scandal when a secret shipment of arms, 500 Thompson SMGs, had been found in a ship bound for Ireland where the customer was the IRA—the Irish Republican Army. And to show how long-lived a Tommy Gun could be, some guns of this type seized from the IRA by the British security forces in the 1970s were traced by their serial numbers to consignments shipped in the 1920s. Suffice to say the Thompson SMG also got an enduring reputation as a favoured weapon of the IRA, right up to modern times, and again it figures in films and books covering the 'troubles' and is known to many by this connection.

Unique reputation

In fact the Thompson SMG must be unique among all classic weapons of war in that it earned its fame first and most enduringly not in any form of military combat but in the hands of others with more furtive motives. Colonel John T. Thompson con-

ceived his famous gun in 1919 and first demonstrated it to the US Army and the New York Police Department in 1920. It was intended for military use, and most specifically for the special demands of trench warfare as a result of World War 1 experience. But by 1920 the military no longer needed such a weapon and defence spending had all but dried up. Neither Thompson nor the company he formed, Auto-Ordnance, ever envisaged anything other than police and military use for the gun. But it took the coming of World War 2, and the frantic needs of nations suddenly at war, to bring the Thompson SMG into military use on the grand scale. Until then it found fame, but in a strictly unconventional way. To see how it was conceived we need to go back to World War 1.

ABOVE: Artist's licence—a decorative heading gets the Thompson SMG detail wrong above a story on the St Valentine's Day Massacre, published in 1929.

BELOW: The special mounting to hold a Thompson SMG for use on police cars, motor cycles, sidecars, and patrol boats. The magazine could be changed without removing the gun from the clamp. Shown is the Type C (100-round) magazine.

A New Type of Weapon

As with so many of the world's most significant weapons, the type of firearm we know today as the submachine gun (SMG) was perfected by German designers first, and German forces were the first to use this type of gun in combat to meet a perceived tactical need. Germany was not the first nation, however, to have a SMG in service, and there were several earlier attempts to develop a rapid-fire hand gun. The machine gun pioneer Hiram S. Maxim developed a small .22in (5.6mm) automatic gun in the 1890s, but it was really more of an automatic pistol with a shoulder stock to give more accuracy and only existed as a prototype. A similar gun was designed by Hugo Borchardt of the Winchester company in 1893; of 7.63mm (.30in) calibre it was actually developed and produced by Mauser. This type of weapon was later taken up by other firms such as Luger and Browning but all were pistols with shoulder stocks, useful but not really significant.

The first rapid-fire automatic rifle-calibre gun was designed by an Italian engineer, Abiel Revelli. It could fire 9mm (0.35in) Parabellum ammunition in sustained bursts of automatic fire. Production was under way in 1915 by the Officine Villar Perosa, but was taken over by Fiat. It was known variously as the Fiat Model 1915, the Revelli, or the Villar Perosa (VP), most commonly the latter. However, the VP was not intended as a hand-held gun. It actually consisted of two guns side by side, each with a 25-round magazine. It had a delayed blowback operation, but a high rate of fire of 1,200-1,500rpm and the magazines could be emptied in one second of continuous fire (effectively 3,000rpm from the two barrels). The weapon was designed to be fitted on the front of motorcycles, combinations, light cars or even bicycles, with or without light armoured shields for the patrol or recce work which was then in

vogue with these light vehicles. It could also be mounted in aircraft turrets or on naval motor boats. A bipod was incorporated. When used by an infantryman, it was rather cumbrously held on a wooden tray supported by a sling round the neck, so it was never very satisfactory as an assault weapon. A sample gun chambered to take .455in (11.6mm) Webley and Scott rounds was tested in 1916 for the British Army but was not taken up, and some manufacture was undertaken in Canada for the Italian Army in 1917-18. Between the wars a single-barrelled much lighter version was developed for infantry use and some of these were still being used in action by Italian troops in World War 2.

German concepts

The armies that marched to war in 1914 were all equipped with well developed and reliable rifles as basic infantry weapons. The German Mauser Gew 38 and British Short Magazine Lee Enfield Mk III were already legendary, even in 1914. They were single-shot bolt-action weapons with magazines loaded from clips. Although heavy and cumbersome by later standards, they had ranges of around 2,000 yards (1,830m) and, with suitable sights, they were excellent for marksman snipers. In well trained hands they were effective weapons and the British, in particular, were famous for their 'ten rounds rapid' (ten rounds in ten seconds) standard of rifle training.

These rifles were perfect for 19th century wars where armies engaged over open ground or formed defensive squares. They were less efficient for the type of warfare that had developed on the Western Front by 1915. Here the opposing armies became bogged down in vast defensive trench systems, and military advances, when there were any, were more often measured in yards than in miles. Often the

LEFT: Luger 08 'Artillery' model showing 'snail' magazine, an early trench warfare weapon.

opposing trench systems were surprisingly close together, only a few hundred yards apart. Aside from the big set-piece offensives, much of the infantry action took the form of reconnaissance patrols or trench raids where a section of enemy trench was attacked, a few prisoners were taken, and as much mayhem as possible was inflicted. In these circumstances the most efficient of rifles had its limitations.

What was needed was a hand weapon that could fire at rapid rate to kill as many men as quickly as possible; it needed to use pistol or revolver calibre ammunition for choice, and had to be light and handy to carry and use. This gave some impetus to the automatic pistol with stock and some of these were made and issued by the Germans, notably the Luger '08 'Artillery' long barrel model that was inspired by Borchardt's original design. This weapon fired 9mm ammunition and had a 32-round 'snail' magazine was fitted to increase the ammunition feed.

This was the starting point for a true rapid-fire gun designed by a leading German ordnance expert whose name would become famous in the next war, Hugo Schmeisser, in 1916 at the Bergmann weapons factory. This gun utilised the same 'snail' ammunition drum and feed as the Luger 'Artillery' pistol, had an air-cooled barrel, and fired from the 'open bolt' position on what became known as the 'blowback' system. In this the firing of the cartridge causes the case to be blown back against the bolt to force it backwards and thus start the firing sequence all over again without pause. This simple idea has never been bettered and remains the principle of operation of most SMGs up to the present day.

Schmeisser's prototype gun was ready for testing early in 1918 and was designated as MP18 (MP = *Maschinen Pistole* = Machine Pistol). With some minor modifications it was rushed into production at the Bergmann factory, now designated MP18,1. This was the gun intended to give the German infantry the edge in trench warfare and over 35,000 were made by the time the war ended in November 1918.

ABOVE: The first practical SMG, the German Bergmann MP18,1, which used the same 'snail' magazine as the Luger 'Artillery' model.

The scale of issue to front line infantry companies was to all officers and NCOs and ten per cent of the men. In each company there was a MP18,1 squad with six guns, six gunners and six ammunition supply men, each of whom retained his Gew 98 rifle. A handcart was issued for every two guns to carry ammunition.

Despite the very short period of use before the war ended, the MP18,1 and the value of a rapid-fire lightweight gun in close-quarter combat made a big impact on fighting men of vision who could see how things might now develop. This was not the case with the higher commands, however. When an intelligence assessment of the MP18,1 was made after tests of a captured weapon in September 1918, the British GHQ in France dismissed suggestions of adopting a similar weapon saying 'no weapon of a pistol nature can ever replace the rifle as the infantryman's main arm . . . No "pistol gun" resembling this particular German weapon is required therefore in the British army'.

Colonel J.T. Thompson

One man of vision who did appreciate what the Germans were doing was Colonel John Taliaferro Thompson, born in 1860, who had retired from the US Army in 1914 after a full career in the US Army Ordnance Department. Among other achievements he had been in charge of the development of the famous M1903 Springfield rifle for the US Army. It was clear to Thompson that American manufacturing skill could be exploited to meet the needs of the warring nations in Europe. Thompson became a consultant to, then chief engineer of, the Remington Arms Co and organised the setting up of two new arms plants, one to make Lee Enfield rifles for Britain and the other to make Moisin-Nagant rifles for Russia.

In addition to this work, Thompson also set out to develop an automatic 'next generation' rifle, a big ambition of his for which he did not anticipate official backing. The automatic action was the key problem: recoil and gas operation methods were too cumbersome and he thought the 'blowback' system, previously used on .22in rifles, would be the answer. However, with the larger rounds of the proposed automatic rifle there would be a need to slow down the action of the breechblock. Thompson found that a US Navy officer, Commander (later Captain) John Blish, had patented a breech delay device in 1915 (originally intended for a pistol) whereby a metal wedge ran up inclined slots under high pressure and jammed to hold the breechblock back. When the pressure dropped the wedge moved back allowing the breechblock to be blown back

To get work started on the automatic rifle Thompson proposed to set up a new company. He offered Blish shares in the concern in return for the use of the Blish patent breech device, and he engaged an old ordnance designer colleague from his army days, Theodore Eickhoff, to do the detailed design work. What Thompson lacked was capital, but his son, Marcellus, himself a US Army artillery officer, was married to the daughter of the former US Ambassador to Great Britain. Through him, Col Thompson was introduced to an influential and successful New York financier, Thomas Fortune Ryan, who had made his fortune in transport, tobacco and rubber. Thompson persuaded Ryan to fund the 'auto rifle' project, as a result of which the Auto-Ordnance Corporation was set up in the summer of 1916 and was formally incorporated in New York in December 1916 with Ryan as President. Marcellus Thompson became Vice-President when he left the US Army at the end of World War 1. Auto-Ordnance did not have its own manufacturing facility: it was a design, development and sales organisation only, and all production, including prototypes, was done by others under contract. Even Theodore Eickhoff, who was designated Chief Engineer of the company, had his offices and experimental workshop at his home town of Cleveland, Ohio, not at the New York HQ. An engineering draughtsman of talent, Oscar V. Payne, applied for a job with the new company and was taken on as assistant to Eickhoff. These two men did all the actual design work on the 'auto rifle' project and on the subsequent developments, but their names are not widely known since the guns produced took Thompson's name as founder of the company. More accurately Col Thompson was the instigator or supervisor of his projects rather than the actual designer.

The United States declared war on Germany on 1 April 1917 and Col Thompson was immediately called back to active service. With his vast experience as an ordnance officer he was promoted brigadier-general and made Director of Arsenals for the US Army, for which work he was later given the US Distinguished Service Medal.

From 'auto rifle' to 'trench broom'
In Thompson's absence, work carried on to perfect the 'auto rifle'. This proved prob-

lematic and work was set back when a round exploded in the chamber because of a malfunction in the Blish locking device. The first job of the newly arrived Oscar Payne in July 1917 was to design a new locking device to prevent the premature locking which had been the cause of the explosion. The 'auto rifle' used the furniture of a Springfield rifle and resembled it in size and shape, except for the breech. It was determined on test that the standard .30in (7.62mm) round, as used in the Springfield, would not work reliably with the automatic bolt of the new gun without being lubricated. One solution considered and suggested was that all .30in rounds should be given wax-coated cartridges. On test this worked, but it added an unwanted complication for field use. Tests with larger calibre rounds suggested that the .45in Pistol Ball round as used in the Colt Model 1911 pistol (which Col Thompson had

BELOW: A US Marine in early jungle fighting, wearing the one-piece camouflaged jungle combat suit, using the M28A1 with the earlier type of simplified backsight. The empty shell cases can be seen in flight from the ejector port.

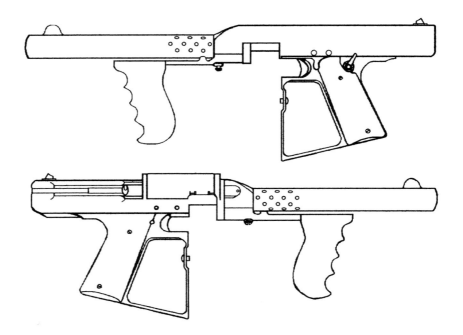

been instrumental in adopting for service in his former army career) was the only round that would work with the automatic bolt without prior lubrication.

Thompson was now in a position, as Director of Arsenals,to get feedback from the US Army Expeditionary Force in France. When Eickhoff communicated the problems with the 'auto rifle' and the commendation to use the .45in round to John Thompson, he got an unexpected reply which changed requirements completely. Thompson's letter said: 'Our boys in the infantry, now in the trenches, need a small machine gun, a gun that will fire 50 to 100 rounds, so light that he can drag it with him as he crawls on his belly from trench to trench and wipe out a whole company single-handed—a one-man hand-held machine gun. A trench broom . . . the Browning machine rifle is too heavy and awkward to handle. I want a little machine

gun you can hold in your hands, fire from the hip, and reload in the dark. You must use the Blish principle and I want it right away. Now go get it. Expense is no object!'

With the troublesome 'auto rifle' no longer a priority, Eickhoff and Payne could start from scratch to design a gun which exactly matched Thompson's brief. By 22 September 1917 Payne could send a drawing to Thompson showing what they proposed. This gun, known as the 'Persuader' to the designers, had no stock or wood furniture, but it did have the pistol grip and forward hand grip that became the hallmark of later Thompson SMGs. It had a simple barrel and breech and a bolt the same diameter as the .45in cartridge. The .45in ACP rounds were belt-fed and empty cartridges were ejected from the top. The bolt pushed the cartridge forward into the chamber to fire it, and this action moved sprockets which advanced the belt to bring the next round into place. The Blish locking system, as modified by Oscar Payne for the 'auto rifle', was incorporated. A safety lever at the top of the pistol grip on the left side allowed the user to select 'safe', 'auto' or 'semi-auto' fire.

The prototype gun was made by Warner & Swasey of Cleveland, but there were immediate problems on test. The belt jammed after firing two or three rounds and

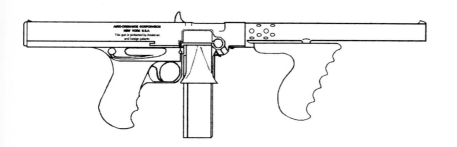

they could never sort this out, concluding the gun was too light for the weight of the cartridges. They decided that heavier components and a box magazine might be the answer and in December 1917 they literally went back to the drawing board.

The redesign was carried out in December 1917 and the new prototype was known to the staff as the 'Annihilator', or 'Annihilator I' when a revised version was built. The 'Annihilator' was similar to the 'Persuader' in terms of barrel and breech, but the pistol grip took the more familiar later shape and a box magazine replaced the belt feed. There was a crude foresight, an actuator handle offset from the line of sight, and the semi-automatic mode was dropped. Rate of fire was 1,500 rpm. Two further improved prototypes were built known as 'Annihilator II'. This revision replaced the barrel cooling sleeve with the familiar cooling fins that also became a hallmark of early Thompson SMGs. The next development, of which about 30 were made, was the 'Annihilator III'. This modification introduced the drum magazine in 20, 50 and 100-round capacities. The eighth gun produced was taken in hand by Oscar Payne to see if its construction could be simplified—he got it down to 11 parts, though the safety lever was eliminated in the process. The ninth gun was less drastically simplified and reduced to 17 parts. However, neither of these simplified guns was entirely satisfactory and this line of effort was dropped. The final guns in this 'Annihilator III' batch added further refine-ments with an attachment point for a stock, a rear sight, a neater magazine release lever with a 'bull's eye' pattern on the end, and actuator knob in the middle of the receiver. All the guns so far made, (about 40 in all) were hand-made in Cleveland using the services of local firms like Warner & Swasey and Sabin Machine Co. This whole series was later called the Thompson Submachine Gun Model 1919, even though they varied in fittings and appearance and were in reality development models.

About 24 guns had been completed by the time the war ended with an Armistice on 11 November 1918 and the balance to a total of about 40 in all were completed in 1919. It was just after the war ended that the name submachine (or sub-machine) gun was dreamed up to describe the new weapon. At first it was going to be called a 'machine gun', but Thompson considered that an inaccurate description as machine guns fired rifle calibre rounds and the new gun fired pistol calibre rounds. The president of Auto-Ordnance Corp suggested it should be the called the Thompson Submachine Gun in honour of the man who conceived the idea, so the gun was thus christened in all further literature and descriptions used by the company.

It was the press who very quickly called it the 'Tommy Gun' and this appellation became so widely used in press reports and everyday speech that Auto-Ordnance Corporation later registered it as a trade name in addition to the full Thompson SMG name.

BELOW: One of the pre-production series Model 1919 guns — No 8. The grip and trigger on this one is towards the rear of the receiver, a variation tried out on this gun. Note the cooling fins on the barrel.

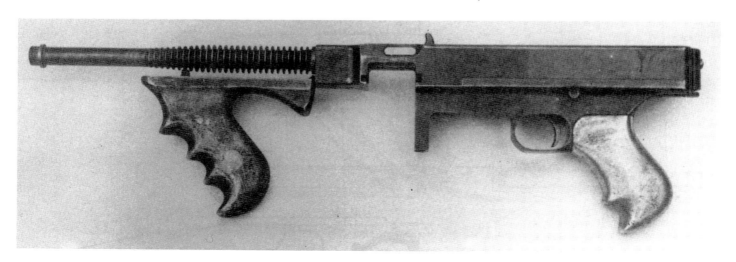

The Thompson SMG in Production

Just as the design had been perfected and the early problems sorted out, the war had ended and with it went any hopes that the gun would be adopted and produced in large numbers for the US Army, since defence spending was immediately reduced and many big contracts were cancelled. To fill in the time while SMG sales were sought, Thompson ordered completion of the 'auto rifle' design. This was done, the lubrication problem for the cartridges being rather crudely overcome by putting oil pads inside the magazine. Various models of the gun were produced in small batches by the Colt Patent Firearms company in 1920-21 under the name of both the 'Thompson Autorifle' and the 'Payne-Colt Autorifle', the latter after the design rights of the gun had been made over to Colt, possibly as part of the deal on SMG production. In 1921 samples were supplied to the US Army for tests but the Test Board, seeking a new semi-automatic rifle for the US Army, rejected the Thompson design largely due to the need for lubricating the cartridge which was considered the worst feature. A 1923 model was produced with a bipod attached to the barrel, but this was also turned down and in 1929 the US Army declared no further interest in it. With the lubrication system of oil pads incorporated, the 'auto rifle' reverted to the use of standard US .30in calibre rounds.

The Thompson SMG was much better received. On 27 April 1920 it was tested by the US Army Ordnance Dept at Springfield Arsenal and impressed by firing 2,000 rounds with only one stoppage. From this test the gun received a good report and this was repeated two or three months later when the US Marine Corps tested it at Quantico. The enthusiasm of the military authorities after these tests encouraged Thompson to get the gun quickly into production. Thompson had good contact with Colt dating back to the development of the Colt M1911 pistol, plus the current work on the 'auto rifle', so it was predictable enough that the production contract would go to this company, whose full name was the Colt Patent Fire Arms Manufacturing

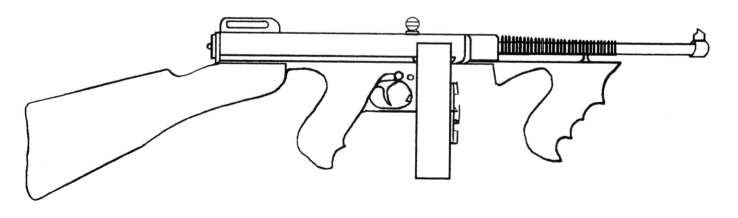

Company. A contract was signed between Auto-Ordnance and Colt on 18 August 1920, which called for production tooling with a capacity to make 100 guns a day, with sufficient components to assemble 15,000 guns and 15,000 magazines. The production was to start six months later and be completed nine months after that. Gun No 26 of the Model 1919 development series was to be used as the production pattern. Auto-Ordnance installed a resident inspector at the Hartford, Connecticut, plant of Colt where the guns were to be made, and he checked all weapons made before they were put into store in the factory warehouse against the time they were sold. The first guns were handed over from Colt to Auto-Ordnance on 30 March 1921, right on contract. There is some evidence, however, that some, at least, of the end of the production run may have been delivered in component form for assembly against orders. The early sales literature offered the gun in alternative versions, against special order chambered for .351in rifle cartridge, 9mm Mauser, 9mm Luger, and .45in Remington rounds as well as the 'standard' .45in ACP round. A stock of components would have allowed for this, though only a few guns in other calibres were ever ordered other than .45in ACP.

The Colt-produced weapon, designated Thompson Submachine Gun Model 1921, was very well made, a quality job. The walnut stock and grips were made by Remington and the sights were made by Lyman Gun Sight Corporation. The gun could fire single shot or automatic and came with a 20-round box magazine as standard. The rate of fire was reduced to 800 rpm and the sights were graduated up to 600 yards (though some demonstrators for overseas customers were marked in metres—600 yards is 550m). The stock was detachable and, as with the Model 1919, the gun could be fired without it. The invoiced price to Auto-Ordnance was $44.56 per gun, including the 20-round magazine which cost 54 cents of the total. Auto-Ordnance in turn quoted a selling price of $180 to $200 to the customer

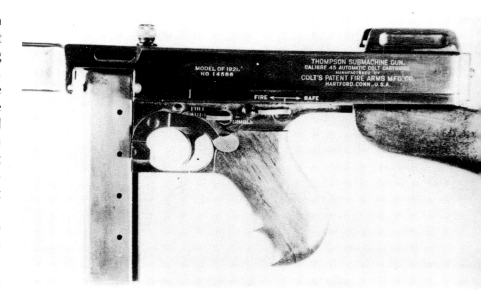

though this had come down to $175 or less by 1923 and dropped lower still later on.

Two of the first four production Model 21s went to the US Infantry School test dept at Fort Benning and the other two went to the US Marine Corps at Quantico. Once again the test reports were enthusiastic, but unfortunately these expressions of approval did not turn into the hoped for orders and the massive 15,000 production run was beginning to look over optimistic. Thompson himself embarked on an extensive demonstration tour of Europe, covering Britain (where he showed it at Bisley), Spain, France, Belgium, Czechoslovakia and Romania. In Britain the gun was examined and briefly tested at Enfield for the benefit of armed services and senior police officers. It performed well except in a rather tough sand test which caused stoppages. The conclusion was that the Thompson SMG was neatly made and easy to handle, and the simplicity of the 20-round box magazine was appreciated. Reservations were expressed over the efficacy of the Blish locking mechanism, but no further tests were called for, nor was any test batch ordered for further evaluation. A few years later, when the Thompson SMG appeared in a British army list of world guns, it was marked as suitable as a police weapon only. The most enthusiastic reception came from the Belgian Army, and in 1924 there was talk of producing 10,000

ABOVE: Close view of the stamped lettering on the left side of the receiver of a Model 1921 gun. This was the standard positioning on all models up to M1928A1.

guns chambered for 9mm Parabellum rounds under licence by FN, but this was never pursued. Most military authorities who showed an interest, including some in South America, at best bought one or two guns to test but these never translated into orders. In the end, however keen the military men were, all governments in the 1920s were keeping defence spending as low as possible and new small arms were very low priority indeed.

The first scandal

While Thompson was on his overseas tour an embarrassing scandal revealed who the first big customer for Thompson SMGs was. The collier *East Side* was in Hoboken, NJ, prior to sailing for Norfolk, Virginia, where she was to load with coal for Ireland. Mysterious new crew members loaded on board packages described as spare parts. Suspicious crew members opened the packets and found guns inside. By the time police arrived and found a total of 495 Thompson SMGs, the new crew members had fled. Police investigation revealed some murky connections with a network of front men and the involvement of American-Irish sympathisers. Though the case never came to court, despite the indictment of Marcellus Thompson and others at Auto-Ordnance, it became known that Thomas Fortune Ryan, the president and main stockholder of the company, was of Irish extraction, a member of Clan Na Gael, and a friend of Irish leader (later President) Eamon de Valera. The guns were destined for the IRA, then headed by Michael Collins, who had been impressed by a secret demonstration of two guns smuggled to Dublin the previous month. These two guns, and three others, made up the total of 500 which constituted the first IRA order, the other 495 being the consignment later confiscated from the *East Side*. General Thompson was not implicated in the deal and had no knowledge of it.

Just four days after the *East Side* consignment was discovered, the first two Thompson SMGs in Ireland were used to ambush a troop train leaving Dublin with incoming British army reinforcements. One gun malfunctioned but the other caused severe damage to the locomotive and wounded three soldiers. It was the only time the Thompson SMG was used in action in that particular period of the 'troubles' because the following month an Anglo-Irish truce was called pending the drawing up of the 1922 peace treaty, after which British forces withdrew from Southern Ireland. This calming down helped the Auto-Ordnance gun-running affair to blow over.

At least four other shipments of Thompson SMGs reached Ireland in the early 1920s, and a few of the Model 1919 pre-production guns may have been among them. Ammunition arrived in quantity, too, and the British army captured 16,000 rounds of .45in ammunition before the guns were first used against them. Further Thompson SMGs made their way to Ireland in later years, including later production and World War 2 models, and various ex-American police weapons. Even guns from the confiscated *East Side* shipment turned up after 1925 when an agent in America bought up the stock in a police sale! There was also a second order for a further 100 Model 1921s, which had not been loaded on the *East Side* and avoided confiscation. Though no definite numbers of Thompson SMGs in the hands of the IRA (or other Irish para-military organisations) is known, they certainly proved long lived, for some guns captured by the security forces in the 1970s proved, by their serial numbers, to have come from the original purchases of the early 1920s over 50 years earlier!

Police and other sales

In the absence of bona fide military sales (and aside from the clandestine supplies to Ireland), the biggest purchasers of the Thompson SMG proved to be the various police forces, sheriff's departments and prison authorities across the United States, plus some of the larger banks and security firms who bought them for their guards. For these markets the company billed the weapon as an 'Anti-Bandit Gun'. The New York Police Department, local to Auto-Ordnance, of course, was the first police purchaser and had nine in the early 1920s. However, police forces in general seem not to have taken to the Thompson until the weapon became a threat in the hands of gangsters from 1926 on. The Chicago police, in the 'front line' of what was by far the bloodiest gangland war in the US, did not make its first purchases until early 1927. By the late 1920s Auto-Ordnance had some assiduous agents who did quite good business travelling around to give demonstrations (and with luck take orders) from different police authorities. Usually policemen who had a chance to fire the gun were impressed and surprised at how easy it was to use. Instead of a shattering hard-to-control weapon which they expected from its reputation or appearance, they found instead a very steady 'user friendly' gun with no nasty recoil and very accurate against close targets.

While the most vicious of the gang fighting died down after Prohibition was repealed in 1933, there were still plenty of bank robbers and hoodlums who used Thompson SMGs through the 1930s, so police forces found it useful to have their own to hand. Surprisingly, the FBI, who played a big part in tracking down 'public enemies' did not get around to adding Thompsons to its inventory until 1935. Nonetheless all these police and law enforcement purchases were mostly in penny numbers and they were slow to reduce the huge stock of guns that Auto-Ordnance had for sale.

An interesting attempt was made to sell SMGs to the US Army Air Corps in the early 1920s, as a weapon for mounting on aircraft. Simulated pressure chamber high altitude tests showed that the Thompson SMG would still fire at a height of over 24,000ft (7,320m). Seven guns were eventually ordered by the USAAC in May 1922 for tests in different fuselage mountings on DH-4B and GA-l aircraft. However, stoppages—so easily dealt with when used by a gunner—could not be cleared when the guns were in remote positions, so use of the Thompson in aircraft was deemed unsuitable. A further test in wing mountings on a DH-4B in 1926 proved even worse, difficulties being experienced both with the remote control linkages and with stoppages. Additionally the .45in round did not have sufficient penetration for aerial attack, so the whole project was abandoned.

BELOW: Model 1923 Military Thompson under test by the US Army in 1924. Note the special features—longer barrel, bipod pivoted on mount, straighter butt, horizontal wood foregrip, and wider magazine for longer cartridges. (See page 20).

RIGHT: Sketch of the Cutts Compensator showing the later production type.

BELOW: Production M1928 for the US Army order of 1938, showing sling swivels, Cutts Compensator and early pattern 30-round box magazine with counting holes. This was later designated M1928A1.

Later variations

Several changes were made to the Thompson SMG between the two world wars. The original M1921, subsequently called M1921A when supplied in standard form, was sold unaltered for some years and the first 3,000 sales were of this type.

Model 1923 Military Thompson

In a further attempt to attract military sales, five M1921 guns were modified to fire the slightly longer .45in Remington round. Apart from rechambering for the new round, this version had a longer barrel with a fitting near the muzzle which could either take a folding bipod or a bayonet. The butt was bulked up, and a grooved front grip replaced the front hand grip. The idea was to turn the weapon into a squad light machine gun. It was demonstrated to a few military authorities and tested by the US Army in 1924, but no orders were forthcoming. Two further guns were modified with the same longer (16in/41cm) barrel and rechambering, but this time without the bipod fitting or the horizontal grooved handgrip—the pistol grip was retained. There was possibly the idea of police sales for this more powerful version, but none were made.

The Model 1923 Military Thompson was also offered with sling swivels for a

sling to meet military requirements. Subsequently this was an option on all models, the suffix S being applied to models so fitted.

Model 1921AC

Col Richard Cutts purchased his own M1921 Thompson and found one weakness of the gun in the hands of an inexperienced firer. With the first shot the muzzle jumped on recoil, and in full automatic it jumped again in rapid succession after every round, faster than the gunner could counter by forcing the muzzle down again. This meant that the gun tended to fire with a rising pattern. Cutts' first attempt to cure this was to fit a counterweight on the muzzle, but this had little effect. A physicist friend studied the problem and suggested an expansion chamber and tube at the muzzle to reduce the recoil by dispersing some of the propellant gases. The slotted unit was simply pushed onto the muzzle in front of the foresight and held in place by a tightened screw. The device was known as the Cutts Compensator and was sold from 1926 as an optional extra, adding $25 to the price. Cutts got a royalty on sales, and the Lyman Gun Sight Corp made it. Many were retrofitted to existing guns. Over the years the Cutts Compensator was itself modified slightly, with the final types fitted on World War 2 guns. There were actually five variants with dimensional differences. The suffix C was subsequently added to all model numbers when the Cutts Compensator was fitted.

Model 1927 Thompson Semi-automatic Carbine

This was also called the Thompson Automatic Carbine Model 27A in Auto-Ordnance catalogues of the time. It was a Model 1921 gun modified to remove the automatic fire selector function so that the gun could only fire in semi-automatic mode (ie, single shots)—hence it was no longer a submachine gun. It was available with or without the Cutts Compensator or sling swivels, and another options was the grooved horizontal foregrip in place of the

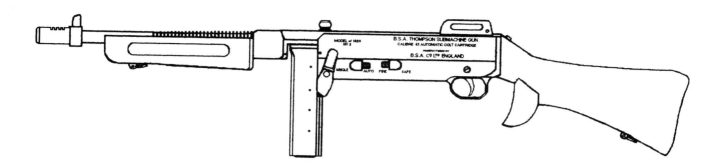

vertical foregrip, this fitting being seemingly derived from the Model 1923. Guns with this feature were described as 'Special Grade' with an S suffix in place of the A—thus Model 27S. A further option offered was the 50-round drum magazine and the suffix D was added to the designation when this was supplied fitted. So it was possible to have a Model 27SCDS indicating: S—a Model 1927 carbine special grade (with horizontal foregrip), C—fitted with Cutts Compensator, D—50-round drum magazine and S—sling swivels.

The 27S was priced more highly than the 27A. On the Model 1927 the original Model 1921 and Thompson Submachine Gun lettering had been ground off the frame and model of 1927) and 'Thompson Semi-automatic Carbine' lettering stamped in its place. This weapon was offered to police forces and prison authorities who did not require the automatic fire facility. Some of these weapons were retrospectively converted back to fully automatic fire function—either officially or otherwise.

Model 1926 BSA Thompson
The Belgian Army had showed great interest in the Thompson SMG on General Thompson's original European tour and carried out field trials in 1923. The Belgians wanted to standardise ammunition on the 9mm Parabellum round, however, and wanted a rifle-style stock and sling. Leading British gun firm BSA (Birmingham Small Arms) had been given the licence for European Thompson sales and Auto-Ordnance asked BSA to remodel the gun for the Belgian requirement. While the frame, box magazine and firing mechanism were all unchanged, the resulting weapon had a plain finless barrel and rifle-style butt and furniture. This was tested by both the French and Belgian armies but in the event no orders were forthcoming, even though the Belgians had mentioned a requirement for 10,000.

Additionally, the French army did not consider the BSA Thompson superior to any available French weapon of similar type.

Model 1929 BSA Thompson
BSA persisted in an attempt to produce a version of the Thompson SMG for the European market. The Model 1929 more closely resembled the American-made models, having the finned barrel, frame, horizontal foregrip, box magazine and firing mechanism identical. However, the butt was of more 'British' shape and there was a conventional rifle-type trigger and trigger guard with a small handgrip behind it, said to improve steadiness when firing from the hip. Versions were produced chambered to take the .45in ACP round,

ABOVE: BSA Thompson of 1929, .45in calibre version.

BELOW: BSA Thompson of 1929, 9mm calibre version.

the 9mm Bergmann round, the 7.63mm Mauser pistol round and the .30in Mauser pistol round. The latter three all had curved box magazines. Cutts Compensators were fitted to all.

Model 1928 Thompson SMG

This was also known as the US Navy Model of 1928 or, more prosaically, the Model 28A. The first big military—to be more precise, government—sale of Thompson guns came unexpectedly in October 1926. A major mail train hold-up took place in New Jersey with a big amount of cash stolen by a gang carrying—and using—Thompson SMGs. The Postmaster-General instantly ordered 200 standard Model 1921A guns from Auto-Ordnance for issue to the US Marines who were called in to guard mail trains against further vicious robberies. The Marine Corps was impressed with these weapons

and, in 1927 when Marines were ordered to sort out insurrections in both Nicaragua and Shanghai, they took some of the M1921As with them and found them ideal for the task. They asked for more, so the US Navy ordered 500, specifying, however, a slower rate of fire. This was done by increasing the weight of the actuator and putting in a much stiffer spring so that the entire action of the gun was slowed down. It reduced the rate of fire from 800 rpm to 600 rpm. The guns were modified from the M1921A stock with the words 'US Navy' stamped on the frame and the 1 of 1921 overstamped with the figure 8.

The guns in this US Navy order had horizontal foregrips, sling swivels and Cutts Compensators. However, the same gun was offered commercially with the vertical foregrip and the other standard options including 50-round drum magazine. Later the original 200 M1921A guns issued to the US Marines were returned to the factory and modified to the same standard.

Following the US Navy order of 1928 the US Army showed interest and ordered 12 Model 1928 US Navy guns for trials. These were tested by the US Cavalry, who decided that they were not suited for mounted regiments due to their short effective range; however, it was felt that the SMGs were useful for auxiliary use in armoured cars (for riot duty, anti-aircraft, patrolling, etc) and recommended they be issued at the rate of one per armoured car. The initial purchase, however, was only 21 guns, and the weapon was standardised for limited procurement as the 'Gun, Submachine, .45 Cal, US Navy Model of 1928', in 1932. The guns delivered to the US Army did not, however, carry the US Navy stamping.

Stocktaking

Apart from the guns themselves, Auto-Ordnance produced numerous accessories for the Thompson SMG. Notable among these was a mounting for sidecar, car scuttle or boat use enabling the gun to be suspended in firing position while still giving access for magazine changing. There were various webbing kits for carrying magazines and slinging guns, and a neat carrying case for housing a disassembled weapon and spare magazines. The magazines available were:

No. of rounds	Magazine	Reference
20	box	Type XX
30	box	Type XXX
50	drum	Type L
100	drum	Type C

Later there was an 18-round box specially for firing a riot cartridge, Type XVIII.

BELOW: The earliest Tommy Guns with the US Army went to armoured vehicles, as demonstrated by the commander of this early production light tank M3A1 in late 1942 or early 1943. The gun is a late M1928A1 with L-type drum magazine.

Despite all the efforts to claw in sales from all quarters, by the end of December 1938, with war in Europe seeming likely sooner or later, only 10,300 of the 15,000 guns made in 1921 had been sold, and there had only been the one production run. Of these guns, the US forces had bought about 1,500, mostly of Model 1928; 4,100 of all models had been sold overseas and the balance had gone to individuals, police and other authorities, etc, in the USA. Thomas Fortune Ryan died in 1929 but his family and the Thompsons carried on the running of the company through the 1930s. The financial state of the company was poor, however, with heavy debts. Early in 1939 a deal was done with an opportunistic industrialist and 'company doctor', Russell Maguire, who took control of a restructured company against heavy debt write-offs. This all happened, of course, at a crucial time in world history.

LEFT: At a training depot in early 1940 crewmen of American M2A3 light tanks defend their position with early M1928A1 Thompsons. Note the L-type drum magazines.

BELOW: Optional bayonet for Models 1923 and 1928.

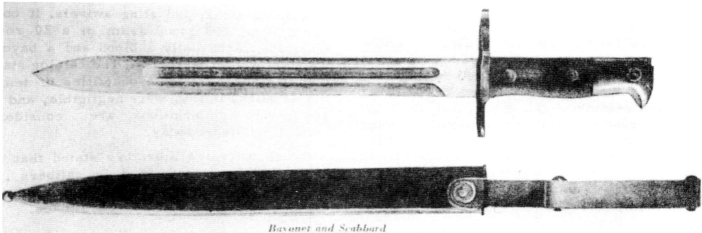

Bayonet and Scabbard

Wartime Production

BELOW: British infantry moving cautiously through Bizerta in May 1943. The first and third men are carrying M1928 Thompsons with vertical fore-grips, probably from the early British orders of 1940-41.

Those countries—Germany, Italy and Soviet Russia—that actively supported the warring factions in the Spanish Civil War of 1936-39 and supplied both weapons and 'volunteer' units, effectively obtained up-to-date battle experience in somebody else's war. This reflected in the weapons they developed and used in World War 2, which started in September 1939: each of these countries saw the value of the sub-machine gun in the infantry assault role and produced new or updated models in quantity.

The nations that stayed aloof from the war seemed to learn nothing from observing it, and both Britain and the United States lacked submachine guns, or any plans to make them, when war started in Europe in 1939. Various examples of sub-machine guns (called 'machine carbines' in those days by the British) were tested in the 1920s and 1930s, including the Revelli, Thompson, Solothurm, Suomi and others. Though reports were submitted each time on their suitability (or otherwise) for British use, the General Staff response was always the same. As late as November 1938 the

ABOVE: British infantry advance through tear gas with Model 1928 Thompsons at a press demonstration of the newly arrived guns in July 1940.

answer was, 'It has been decided not to introduce a weapon of this nature into the British Army. Work on the design of a machine carbine can therefore be closed down.' This was said when Britain was already rearming after the Munich Crisis. Several of the responses and reports by British commanders in the 1930s refer to SMGs as 'gangster' guns: 'we have no need for gangster guns in the British army' was a typical response, which reflects, perhaps, the notoriety that the Tommy Gun had received in the hands of American gangsters and the many gangster films. As is often the case, no doubt, the 'not invented here' factor was also involved in these reactions,

The result was that the soldiers of the British Expeditionary Force went to France in September 1939 armed with the Short Magazine Lee Enfield rifle (as in 1914) and light and heavy machine guns, but without any submachine guns, a type widely used by their German foes. Predictably enough, by December 1939 the BEF was calling for

LEFT: Home Guard sergeant with a late production Thompson M1928A1, probably at the Home Guard Training School, Richmond Park, Surrey, in 1942. Note the horizontal foregrip, 30-round box magazine, regular sling and Cutts Compensator.

RIGHT: US Army infantry sergeant poses with the latest American infantry weapons, in a display in December 1941 immediately after the United States was pulled into World War 2. He is holding a very recently made Thompson M1928A1 with the horizontal foregrip standardised in all new production only eight months previously.

'an immediate supply of machine carbine or gangster guns'. The various SMGs that had been purchased for tests in the inter-war years, one of them a Thompson SMG, were sent to France for troop trials. Given the urgency, and the fact that some of the guns were unobtainable from countries (like Finland with the Suomi) now at war, it was concluded that the Thompson SMG was the only one that was easily available, though it was not considered the best choice. Also it involved dollar exchange and was the most expensive gun (at £50 each, Cutts Compensator extra) of all those tried. During 1940 a copy of the German Bergmann MP28 was made and put into production as the Lanchester, but this was overtaken by the much superior British-designed Sten gun which went into production a year later and was much preferred by the British army. The Lanchester production was therefore passed to the British Royal Navy who used these rather heavy and 'antique' SMGs well into the 1960s.

Until the Sten gun was ready in substantial numbers, the Thompson SMG from USA admirably filled the gap. A British Purchasing Mission to USA had been set up in November 1939 charged with buying as many weapons as were needed (or obtainable) from the United States. Its purchases covered every conceivable item of ordnance and the first order for Thompson SMGs in answer to the British Army's request was placed on 1 February 1940, for 450 pieces. This was not the first overseas order, since the French Purchasing Mission had ordered 3,750 in December 1939. These low figures probably related to what was in stock and could be supplied immediately for they come close to the 4,700 stock figure of late 1938. The French placed a further order for 3,000 guns and the British placed orders totalling 107,500 by the end of 1940. Another order in 1940 came from the Swedish Army.

With the coming of war in Europe and plenty of overseas custom in prospect, plus the start of rearmament in the USA itself, the new management of Auto-Ordnance Corporation was now faced with the problem of supply. The stock that had sufficed for nearly 20 years was going fast and new production was needed. Colt, the original contractor, could not help because the company was also inundated with other ordnance contracts, so the Savage Arms Corporation was asked to contract for the work in December 1939, the requirement being 10,000 of the Model 28A (Model 1928). Problems arose at once when it came to finding all the tooling from 1921 and getting the supply of it from Colt, and there were snags with butts and sights. New tooling was necessary before production could begin. A further contract for 3,500 guns followed in April 1940. Production was under way by the spring of 1940 at Savage's Utica plant in New York state, and thereafter orders followed at frequent intervals—100,000 were placed by the end of 1940. By the end of 1940 orders totalling 20,450 guns had come in from the US Army for delivery in 1941. Unfortunately General John Thompson, now long retired, died in June 1940 so he barely lived long enough to see his brainchild produced in numbers exceeding anything he had dreamed of back in 1918.

With even bigger orders in prospect, Russell Maquire, the Auto-Ordnance owner, sought extra production facilities and, presumably to keep outgoings down, it was decided that Auto-Ordnance would have its own plant. An old brake shoe factory was purchased in Bridgeport, Connecticut, and some necessary tooling was rounded up. Some of it was old equipment from World War 1 leased from government arsenals, and a notably 'historic' piece was a Pratt & Whitney profile miller dating from the American Civil War that had been used in musket production. The premises were acquired in August 1940 and were in full production exactly one year later. In fact only a few parts were actually made in this factory: it assembled the guns from components contracted out to others. Remington was the most important sub-contractor as it supplied the barrels and firing mechanisms. During World

BELOW: American Jeep crew respond to an ambush during an exercise in Australia late 1942. The gun is an early M1928A1 with the Cutts Compensator and still with the original graduated backsight.

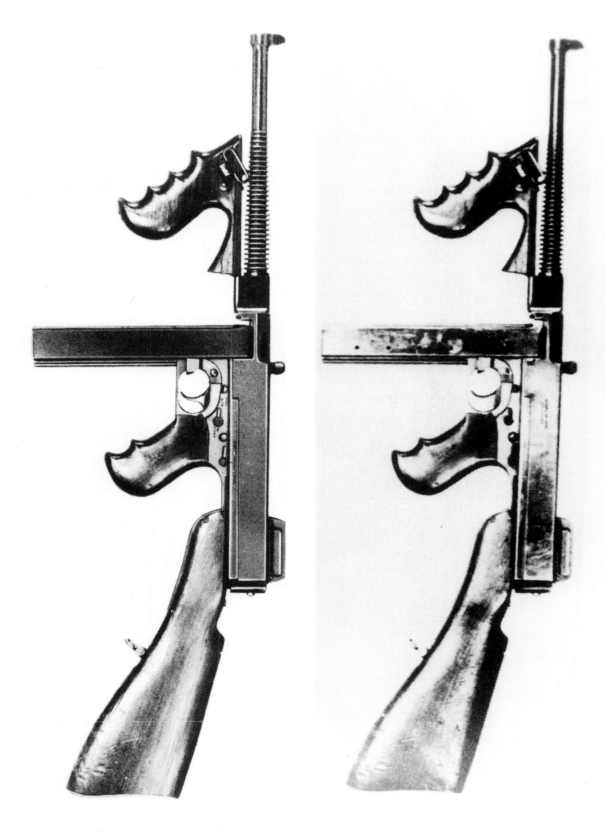

ABOVE LEFT: Thompson M1928A1 showing original backsight, finned barrel, vertical foregrip, 30-round box magazine, and sling swivels.

ABOVE RIGHT: Thompson M1928A1 with the earlier type of 30-round box magazine featuring counter holes to show how much ammunition is left. These holes were eliminated when combat conditions caused dirt/sand to get inside and jam the feed.

War 2 Thompson guns produced by Savage had an S prefix in front of the serial number, and guns from the Auto-Ordnance plant had an A.O.

Contracts to the Savage company alone in 1941 amounted to no fewer than 275,000 guns; after the first 50,000 the vertical foregrip was abandoned completely in favour of the wood-grooved horizontal foregrip which was used on all models from then on. Savage orders for 1942 amounted to 500,000, and in 1943 over 360,000. Production figures overall were huge whichever way you look at them. Total orders placed by the US Ordnance Dept for US forces alone totalled 1,387,134 units of all models combined. Until the Lend-Lease Act of March 1941, all the British and other overseas orders had to be paid for on a 'cash and carry' basis. This would have included over 18,000 Thompsons ordered by the Australian Army in January 1941. The actual numbers

ordered and received by Britain are difficult to quantify but are said to cover the bulk of 1940-41 production outside US Army requirements. This would be in excess of 300,000 guns, but against that up to 100,000 were said to have been lost in ships sunk in Atlantic convoys, and some of the numbers after Lend-Lease came into force may have been diverted from US Army orders. Lend-Lease guns also went to the Chinese Army and all the Allied armies, including such as the Free French and Polish forces in Britain, although some of their guns probably came from British deliveries.

Production modifications

The story of the Tommy Gun during World War 2 is one of several changes of both detail and model in order to simplify and speed up production, and keep costs down. By the standards of the 1940s it was not a good production proposition. It was

ABOVE: An interesting comparison showing two different models of the Thompson SMG used by men of the 82nd Airborne Division in Normandy, June 1944. On the left is a M1928A1 of early production type with finned barrel, Cutts Compensator and Lyman backsight; and on the right is a M1A1 with plain barrel, simplified pressed metal backsight, and reinforcing bolt through the heel of the butt.

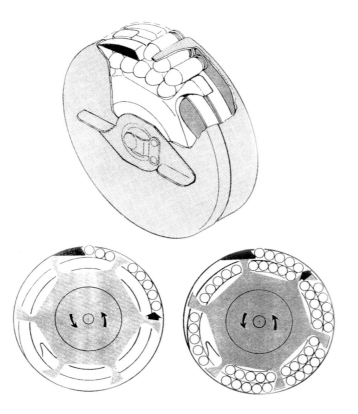

ABOVE: Cross-section and construction of drum magazine, Type L (50-round) showing spiral feed and star rotor.

an elegant design, but needed far too much engineering and assembly work, in contrast to the much cruder guns like the Sten and M3 that were designed after 1940. Design development is best described model by model.

Gun, Submachine, Calibre .45, Model of 1928A1

This was the official US Army designation after it was rated as a standard weapon in September 1938, with a purchase of 400 units. It was, in fact, the army's name for the M1928 Navy Model, the same as had been supplied to the US Navy for use by the Marines as previously described, the only difference being the stamping of the new designation 'US MODEL 1928A1' on the receiver instead of the Navy designation. The original 400 went to armoured and recce units (motorcyclists, armoured cars, half-tracks, etc). The subsequent 1940-43 orders of this type amounted to 562,511 units.

In December 1941 the US Army standardised on the 30-round box magazine as the only one to use, after tests showed it the best of all the magazine options available. Simplification took place to the gun itself during 1941. Changes included:

- elimination of the adjustable back-sight in favor of a simple peepsight
- machined ejector replaced with a fabricated stamped one
- cooling fins altered from rounded to squared off
- walnut butt and woodwork replaced with cheaper grades of wood
- from March 1941 the vertical foregrip was replaced with the horizontal grooved-wood foregrip, and sling swivels were fitted to all guns—previously this was an optional extra that had to be retro-fitted unless specified in the order

Some earlier M1928A1 models incorporated some, or all, of these changes when they were overhauled or repaired. Elimination of the Lyman rearsight came last of all in December 1941, its replacement being a simple pressing with two distinctive 'wings'.

Gun, Submachine, Calibre .45, Thompson M1

The M1928A1 was costing too much to make ($59 unit price in 1941) and in order to reduce the cost, even after the simplifications, the Chief Engineer of the Savage plant at Utica, John Pearce (who was English), got together with a designer from the Stevens arms company to produce a radical rethink of the gun during November and December 1941. On the revised design, the Blish locking device was eliminated, the barrel cooling fins were omitted (resulting in a plain, smooth, barrel), the Cutts Compensator was omitted, the stock was non-detachable, only the box magazine could be fitted, and the sights were simplified to give a metal pressing peepsight at the back. The blowback arrangement, one-piece bolt, firing pin and hammer remained unchanged from the M1928, as did the trigger and other internal parts. The bolt was moved to the right side and the firing selector and safety levers were changed to flat machined strips, but later were changed again to metal pins.

Absence of the Blish locking device was found not to affect performance and the

LEFT: Early production Thompson M1A1 with sling fitted and the original simplified backsight. Later production had the improved pressed metal backsight with 'wings' and a reinforcing bolt through the heel of the butt.

BELOW LEFT: American soldier at Altenberg, close to the German border, checks the blown up river bridge, carrying his Thompson M1A1. This has the reinforcing band commonly added round the foregrip and barrel on the late models.

BOTTOM: Late production Thompson M1A1 showing 30-round box magazine, simplified rearsight. and pin-type safety and firing levers.

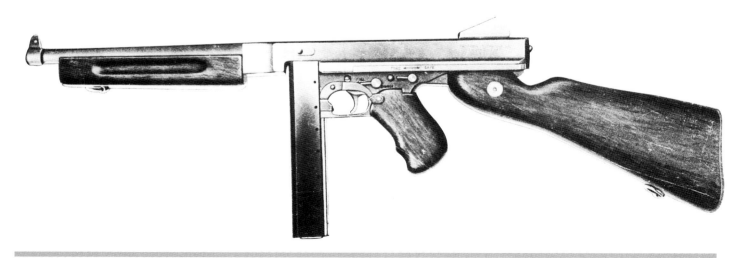

RIGHT: Manufacturing .45in calibre bullets, with the slugs being cut from a reel of lead wire. Over four billion were made in World War 2.

BELOW: US Rangers training for the Normandy landings in 1944, and carrying M1 or M1A1 guns with 30-round box magazines.

prototype gun fired 10,000 rounds without a stoppage. This prototype was completed in February 1942 and sent for test to the US Ordnance Dept in March. It was tested, approved and standardised in April 1942, such was the pace of events brought on by the war, which had involved the United States, too, since December 1941. The Savage company made no royalty claim on what was a major revision and production of the new M1 started in June 1942 at both the Savage and Auto-Ordnance plants, replacing the M1928A1 completely in production. Some were also produced at the Stevens plant.

Gun, Submachine, Calibre .45, Thompson, M1A1

The final production version of the Thompson SMG was approved for manufacture in October 1942 when it was standardised after tests. In fact, there was only one simple production change, whereby the firing pin and hammer on the bolt were discarded in favour of a firing pin in the form of a stud integral with the bolt face. Externally it is difficult to tell an M1 and M1A1 apart aside from the stamped designation on the receiver—additionally some M1s and M1A1s had the firing pins interchanged when repaired. A modification applied to many guns on overhaul was a metal binding band round the front of the foregrip and the barrel to reinforce the fixing, but this was not a factory fitting. Also a bolt was put through the heel of the butt to strengthen it.

Total numbers of M1 Thompsons produced were in 1942-43, 285,480, and of M1A1s in 1943-44, 539,143. The unit price of these models came down to $33-36.

All Thompson SMG production ceased in December 1944 and the plants engaged in their production were switched to other weapons work by order of the US Ordnance Department. This run down and termination of production was announced in spring 1943 when the much simpler M3 'Grease Gun' was chosen as the new standard SMG for the US Army

Test guns and prototypes

Very many one-off and test pieces were made based on Thompson SMGs, some with a view to production, others to test possible production modifications. Among the more interesting was a version of the M1 with a cocking handle on both sides. On the production M1 and M1A1 the cocking handle was on the right, which made it awkward to cock since it had to be tilted over to the left unless the right hand could be used. This modification was not taken up.

The Savage company made at least one prototype of a modified M1928A1 chambered to take 9mm Parabellum ammunition from a curved magazine. Experiments in 1943 led to 40 M1928 pattern guns with aluminium receivers and plastic moulded handgrips, and in two cases plastic butts.

In about 1941 Auto-Ordnance made six guns of the M1928A1 type with stainless steel receivers. Marked as 'Thompson Submachine Gun, Calibre .45' M1A2, US Navy, this was possibly to test the feasibility of combating corrosion at sea. In late 1942 a Thompson M1928 was modified and rechambered to take .30in calibre rounds as a possible 'short rifle' or 'carbine' M1 for the US Army, though it was not taken up.

Ammunition and accessories

The standard cartridge used in all models of the Thompson SMG was the .45in ACP: this, as the designation implies (ACP = Automatic Colt Pistol), was the cartridge already developed for the Colt M1911 Pistol, a weapon that was already in service when the SMG was conceived. John Thompson had been involved in the development, testing and adopting of the M1911 for the US Army during his career with the Ordnance Dept. The bullet weighed 230 grains (7,000 grains = one pound), one of the heaviest pistol calibre bullets produced. Used in the Thompson SMG it had a muzzle velocity of 920ft/sec (280m/sec) which made it relatively slow against other SMGs. However, it had excellent stopping power at close range, and was most effective up to about 100 yards (90m). Beyond that, accuracy fell off sharply and the graduation on the backsight up to 600 yards (550m) was a trifle optimistic.

With so many Thompson SMGs in use, ammunition requirements were very high and total production of .45in calibre ACP cartridges in the 1940-45 period amounted to 4,072 million rounds, though these were also intended for pistol and revolver use, of course, and also for the M3 'Grease Gun' which replaced the Thompson SMG in production.

Also available for the Thompson SMG was a blank cartridge and several types of cartridge for 'riot control'. The birdshot cartridges had a 'paper' bullet containing 108 or 130 pellets for use up to a range of 50 yards (46m). There was also a 'multiple slug' cartridge containing a ballshot in the nose and three lead discs in a thin gilt metal housing. A special box magazine of 18-round capacity was produced for use with shot cartridges dimensioned and sprung to prevent the noses of the rounds being crushed or damaged while loading. This magazine was designated Type XVIII. Finally there was also an inert dummy round for drill and instructional purposes.

For the Model 1923 a special 45in calibre Remington cartridge was developed (known as the .45in Remington-Thompson). This weighed 250 grains (against the 230 grains of the standard round) and the cartridge case was 0.12in (3mm) longer. The idea was to give higher muzzle velocity. The gun had to be specially chambered for the longer cartridge and a re-dimensioned magazine was also required. However, due to the commercial and military failure of the Model 1923, this cartridge must have seen very limited demand and it was dropped in 1931.

The feature of the Thompson SMG that gave it much of its sinister and dramatic character was the drum maga-

Counter Intelligence corpsmen examine a dead Japanese soldier at Saipan on 26 January 1944. The man on the left carries a Thompson M1 or M1A1 in the approved manner.

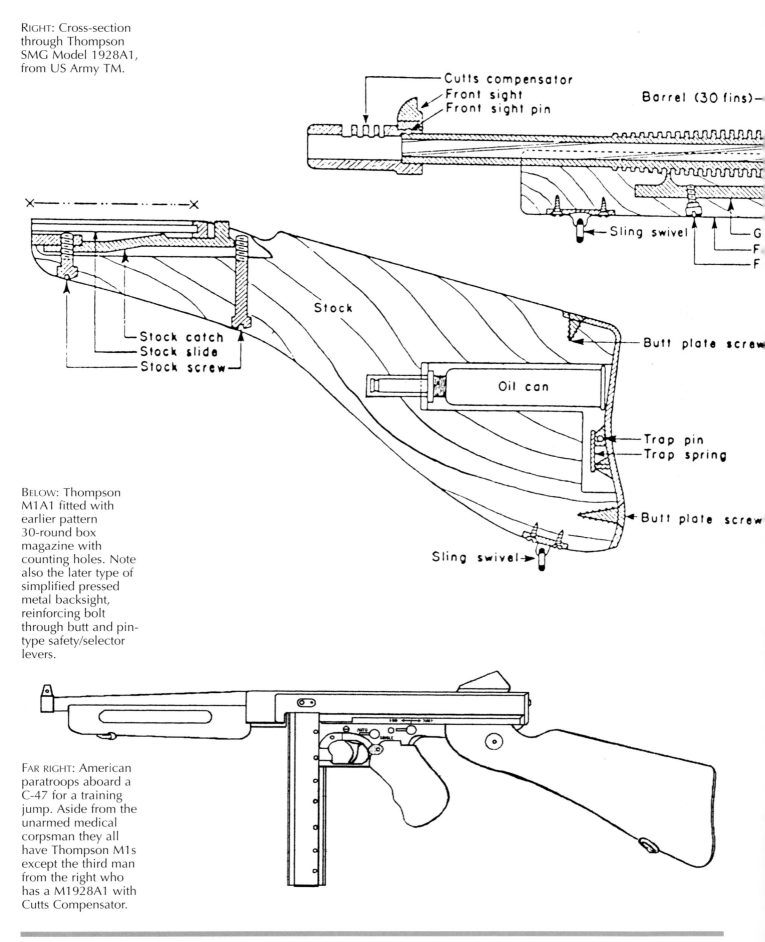

RIGHT: Cross-section through Thompson SMG Model 1928A1, from US Army TM.

Cutts compensator
Front sight
Front sight pin
Barrel (30 fins)

Sling swivel

G
F
F

Stock catch
Stock slide
Stock screw

Stock

Oil can

Butt plate screw

Trap pin
Trap spring

Butt plate screw

Sling swivel

BELOW: Thompson M1A1 fitted with earlier pattern 30-round box magazine with counting holes. Note also the later type of simplified pressed metal backsight, reinforcing bolt through butt and pin-type safety/selector levers.

AUTO
SINGLE

FAR RIGHT: American paratroops aboard a C-47 for a training jump. Aside from the unarmed medical corpsman they all have Thompson M1s except the third man from the right who has a M1928A1 with Cutts Compensator.

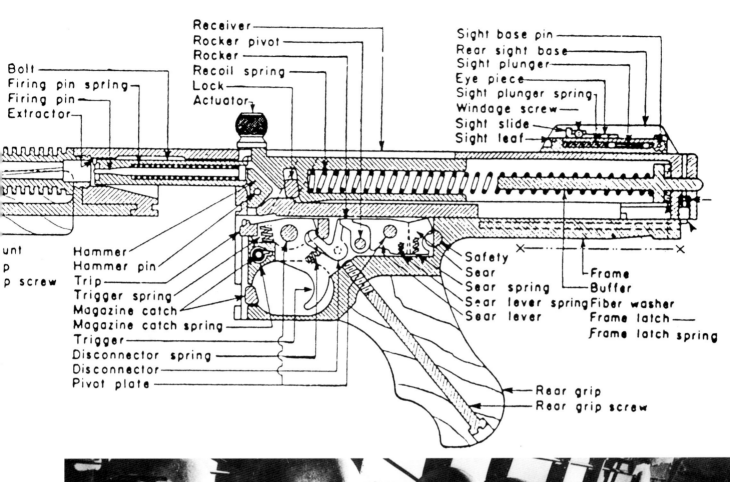

Bolt
Firing pin spring
Firing pin
Extractor
Receiver
Rocker pivot
Rocker
Recoil spring
Lock
Actuator
Sight base pin
Rear sight base
Sight plunger
Eye piece
Sight plunger spring
Windage screw
Sight slide
Sight leaf

unt
p
p screw

Hammer
Hammer pin
Trip
Trigger spring
Magazine catch
Magazine catch spring
Trigger
Disconnector spring
Disconnector
Pivot plate

Safety
Sear
Sear spring
Sear lever spring
Sear lever

Frame
Buffer
Fiber washer
Frame latch
Frame latch spring

Rear grip
Rear grip screw

FAR RIGHT: US Army MP checks for booby traps in Isigny, Normandy, on 16 June 1944. He carries an early M1928A1 Thompson with the Cutts Compensator and 20-round box magazine (Type XX). On his waist belt he has a standard issue five-section pouch for the 20-round box magazine.

BELOW: The five-section pouch and belt for carrying magazines. This was produced in both commercial and US Army forms.

zine. Though, superficially, all these look alike, there were actually several types. The most widely used was the 50-round drum, known as Type L. Though there were some development prototypes, the final arrangement used a star-shaped rotor driving the cartridges round a spiral ramp. The rotor had a spring which was 'wound up' when the drum was loaded with rounds through the feed aperture. A small winding key was fitted externally on the centre of the rotor axle. The Model 1921 types required an 11-click wind, and the Model 1928 types required nine-clicks because of the reduced rate of fire. An instruction plate for this was affixed on the faceplate of the drum. Several different firms produced drums, particularly when orders increased in 1940-41, leading to minor variations in detail, such as instruction plate shape and fixing, and the number of drain slots (which allowed the 'blueing' solution to drain off when the drums were finished). In 1941 the US Ordnance Dept tested a Bakelite Type L drum with a view to saving metal, but this proved too fragile and was not adopted.

The other option offered was the 100-round drum known as Type C (easy to remember in Roman numerals—C = 100, L = 50). This worked the same way as the 50-round drum but needed 15 clicks when reloading. It weighed 4.95lb (2.25kg) against 2.63lb (1.2kg) for the 50-round drum. Type C drums were not produced in the same huge quantities as the Type L, the weight, price and more frequent stoppages

experienced being against them. Production of the C drum was discontinued early on and it was not offered as an option on the Model 1928 gun.

The most commonly used magazine was the 20-round box Type XX, which was the standard supply with the gun in most cases. It was easy to make, and a spring under compression in the bottom of the box maintained the supply of cartridges into the chamber. Several firms produced Type XX magazines, leading to minor variations of finish and lettering, etc. A wider box magazine for shot cartridges only was designated Type XVIII for 18 rounds, as noted above. A 30-round magazine, Type XXX, was also offered, and this became the only type produced from the end of 1941. Again there were minor differences in the trim, finish and lettering, due to different firms making them. An idea introduced by US paratroops in 1944 was to tape two box magazines together, back-to-back and end-to-end, so that when the first magazine was empty, the assembly was turned to insert the second magazine with minimal delay.

There were numerous types of carrying gear for the Thompson SMG, included several different canvas satchels: one style for the US Army was intended to allow the gun to be carried vertically slung from a cavalry saddle. Some equipment was designed by the US Army, but Auto-Ordnance also offered canvas cases, pouches for cleaning gear, and pouches and belts for carrying both box and drum type magazines. The US Army had pouches for carrying both 20-round and 30-round magazines, and there was a British army pouch for carrying Type L drums. Auto-Ordnance, and others, sold hard briefcase and attache case containers of various sorts and degrees of quality for carrying the gun, ammunition, cleaning gear and spare magazines.

Silencers could easily be fitted to the Thompson though they were not offered by the factory. Different types of silencer were attached, and in World War 2 they were mostly used by special forces on covert operations. Flashguards could similarly be fitted.

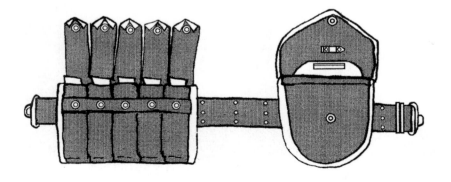

Tommy Gun in Service

ABOVE: All the Allies used the Thompson, including these Kachin Tribesmen recruited locally as units to aid the British and US forces in North Burma. The nearest man here, in early 1945, has a M1928A1 gun.

RIGHT: An Indian soldier in Burma carries a late production M1928A1 Thompson with Cutts Compensator, no barrel cooling fins, and the earlier form of simplified backsight.

The Thompson SMG had the distinction of being used, liked and favoured by all sides in World War 2. Despite its shortcomings in terms of bulk, short effective range and poor accuracy, it was pleasant and satisfying to handle, fell to hand easily and was highly reliable. Stoppages were rare and, when they did occur, were easy to clear. The gun worked well in all weathers and temperatures though it had to be kept clear of sand ingress. Above all the Thompson had great stopping power, which was an

important consideration in close-quarter warfare. A veteran of the Burma campaign told the author that the Tommy Gun was a much prized possession in jungle fighting, even if not on official issue to the unit, since a round 'would knock down the enemy even if it only hit his little finger'.

The first users in World War 2 seem to have been the French in the early months of 1940, though at least one Thompson, and possibly more acquired from private sources in England, was tested in France before the British withdrawal in May 1940. It was from the 'Phoney War' period that the message was first passed back that the drum magazine was unsatisfactory for military use since the ammunition 'clinked' in it and night patrols on the Saar front drew German fire when this sound gave away their position. Hence the box magazine was standardised, but not before thousands of drum magazines had been issued anyway with early deliveries of Thompson guns to the British forces.

The first Thompsons from the initial British orders arrived in July 1940 as Britain 'stood alone' against the threat of German invasion. Fair publicity was given to the availability of this fierce looking weapon at the time, for reasons of public morale and propaganda. The new Home Guard units were shown training with them, as were

units of the regular army. In reality the issue was rather thinly spread from the initial deliveries. Only Home Guard units in the south and south-east, near possible invasion points, had the guns and then only as one or two per unit. Other guns were put into caches for the Home Guard units that were designated to go 'under cover' to conduct guerrilla warfare if the Germans actually landed.

Prime Minister Winston Churchill, touring anti-invasion defences in the summer of 1940, inspected a unit which had Thompsons and famously posed with one for the press in pictures that went around the world symbolising British defiance against Hitler. Nazi propagandists saw the old Chicago connections at once and used the same picture to brand Churchill as a 'gangster' showing that the Thompson's old notoriety had still not been forgotten.

When the British 'special forces' units—commandos and paratroops—started to train and form in 1941, they were extensively equipped with Thompson SMGs and pictorial evidence suggests that airborne units had extra Thompsons replacing some rifles, but not the Bren guns, in platoons. An early British modification for the Paratroop Thompsons was the repositioning of the sling swivels on the top of the butt and the left side of the foregrip so that the gun could be slung horizontally from the shoulder and carried with the muzzle pointing down.

In other fighting units the Thompson was issued to rifle-section commanders and NCOs, and armoured unit troops, etc. When the Sten gun was put swiftly into production in 1941 as the new standard issue British SMG it replaced the Thompson quite quickly with front line units, but the Tommy Gun was still to be seen in service right up to the end of the war. It was particularly favoured for jungle fighting in the Far East and was preferred to the Sten gun by many units in the east.

The original pattern of parachute harness used by British airborne forces had special slings incorporated into which a Thompson SMG fitted when jumping.

ABOVE: The famous picture of Prime Minister Winston Churchill posing defiantly with a Tommy Gun, late summer 1940. The weapon is a standard Model 1928 from the early British orders, fitted with a Type L magazine and Cutts Compensator. Visible are the barrel fins, the ejector port and the folded backsight.

LEFT: The first type of British paratroop harness incorporated a sling to carry the Thompson SMG while jumping as this exhibition display shows. The gun here is a late production M1928A1 without the sling fitted.

RIGHT: Early days of the Parachute Regiment; a line-up ready for a demonstration jump on 21 October 1941 with M1928 Thompsons prominent (and Bren guns) carried by the nearest troops. Men to the rear carry rifles.

BELOW: Crew and passengers of a damaged Waco Hadrian glider wait to be picked up on a Burmese landing ground, the two nearest men being equipped with M1A1 Thompsons. The method of slinging across the back, magazine upwards, was common with US forces.

Men of the 29th Ranger Battalion training in England on l2 July 1943. On the left a Browning Automatic Rifle M1918A2 and on the right a Thompson SMG M1928A1, late production with smooth barrel, horizontal foregrip, and Cutts Compensator.

RIGHT: A soldier of 82nd Airborne Division climbs aboard a C-47 for the drop in France, early morning of 6 June 1944, with his Thompson M1 strapped into his parachute harness.

BELOW: US Army rifle squad house-clearing in Brest in 1944 are surprised by an exploding phosphorus shell. The squad leader in the centre carries a Thompson M1.

Like the British, the US Army had given no great thought or priority to the provision of a submachine gun prior to 1940. Even though the Thompson SMG had been standardised by the US Army in 1938, only enough guns were purchased to equip armoured forces, but with the expansion of the army and a study of German tactics it was realised that a squad weapon was needed, and the Thompson SMG filled the need largely because it was developed and in production already. There was no time to develop anything else, though efforts to produce a better, more easily made, replacement did start, resulting in the M3 'Grease Gun' to supplant the Thompson in production from 1944. The Thompson was seen in use by all arms throughout World War 2 and was generally universally liked. There were exceptions, though. On Guadalcanal the US Marines withdrew all their Thompsons from service and relied solely on the BAR as a squad automatic weapon. This was because the Thompson sounded too much like a Japanese machine gun and brought down friendly fire on several occasions. In contrast, US Army troops in Papua dumped their BARs as being too heavy to carry and maintain in the jungle and they replaced them with more Thompsons instead. A general complaint from commanders in the campaign against the Japanese was the huge expenditure of ammunition caused by poor fire discipline

ABOVE: Many Thompson SMGs were among the weapons delivered to the Chinese Army. Here in December 1943, at a training camp in India, two late production M1928A1s are visible in the front rank of this company under training with an American instructor.

in the jungle. One complained of '. . . wild and prolonged firing at imaginary targets or no targets at all.' The Thompson made this all the easier.

Apart from the early batch of Tommy Guns purchased by France, others went to Russia and Yugoslavia in 1941 under Lend-Lease. The German Army captured many of the French Thompsons when they conquered France in June 1940, and then they captured further quantities of guns and ammunition when they invaded Russia and Yugoslavia. Further stocks were captured from the British and Commonwealth forces in the Western desert campaign of 1941-

42. Sufficient material was held for the weapon to go on issue as the MP 760 (f) or (r) or (j) and it was seen in some numbers in German hands, where it also proved popular.

Large numbers of M1928A1 and M1/M1A1 Thompson SMGs were also supplied to Chiang Kai-Shek's Chinese army, a major ally in the fight against Japan. All Commonwealth armies, plus the 'free' forces from conquered Europe, were users of the gun, the latter most often coming from British stocks since most of these forces were based in Britain.

LEFT: Driver of an Afrika Korps VW Kübelwagen checks his captured Tommy Gun, in the Western Desert, summer 1942. The gun is a M1928 with 50-round drum and Cutts Compensator, but no front sling swivel.

RIGHT: Men of the US 7th Army in white snow camouflage smocks extemporised from sheets, patrol a wood south of Bitche, near Strasbourg, in January 1945. The first and fourth man in this squad carry M1 or M1A1 Thompsons

BELOW: The Thompson M1A1 in service, held by a squad leader in an infantry platoon of 82nd Airborne Division aboard a Hadrian glider during training for D-Day. The other men have rifles and a bazooka.

LEFT: Standard Thompson M1 or M1A1 used by a US corporal during house searches at Wiltz, Luxembourg, in winter 1944-45.

BELOW: German soldiers surrender to men of the US 9th Army in November 1944 near Geilenkirchen. The furthest man has a Thompson M1.

ABOVE: Men of 101st Airborne Division move past dead colleagues in a field near Carentan on 14 June 1944. The two nearest men have Thompson M1s or M1A1s.

RIGHT: The original M28A1 Thompson stayed in service right through the war. This M1928A1 with 50-round drum magazine is being used by a Marine at Bourgainville in November 1943. In front is a light tank M3A1.

FAR RIGHT: A squad leader peers cautiously round the corner in the village street of Thimister, 11 September 1944, near the Belgo-German border. He is carrying a Thompson M1A1. The men behind have M1 carbines.

Rivals and Successors

BELOW: The Hyde-ATMED SMG prototype.

Though the US Ordnance Dept placed huge orders for the Thompson SMG in 1940, and standardised the M1928A1's successors—the Thompson M1 and M1A1—very quickly in order to maintain supply in a time of need, there was an awareness that this was not the ideal design, either in terms of cost or in its features. In February 1941 the Ordnance Department invited submission of new designs for selection as a standard SMG, the brief being that it should be adapted for cheap and simple production and that it could be capable of adaptation for .45in calibre or 9mm calibre ammunition with minimal change of parts.

Even before this, however, several possible SMG designs had been tested by the Ordnance Board, either called in or submitted by their designers or makers. These included the following:

Hyde Model 35

This was designed by George Hyde who had come to USA from Germany in 1926. A gunsmith and designer by profession, he offered his latest prototype, the Model 35, to the US Army for consideration in 1939. This was a close look-alike to the Thompson Model 1921 but had several differences, including a tubular receiver and a cocking lever right at the back of this housing. Three 20-round box magazines could be joined together and moved across the feed slot as ammunition was expended. The gun was tested by the US Army in October-November 1939, but high muzzle flash, weaknesses of construction, and the position of the cocking lever told against it even though in some respects it was better than the Thompson M1928. It was not taken up.

Hyde ATMED SMG

Superficially this gun like the Thompson M1928A1 of late production with the horizontal wood foregrip. It was designed by Hyde and made by the ATMED Manufacturing Co. It was intended for possible commercial sale. It was submitted to the US Army for test but suffered numerous misfires and stoppages on test, particularly when used with military ammunition (less so with commercial ammunition). It performed particularly well in a mud test, but overall it was not considered worth further tests. Consequently only a very few were ever made.

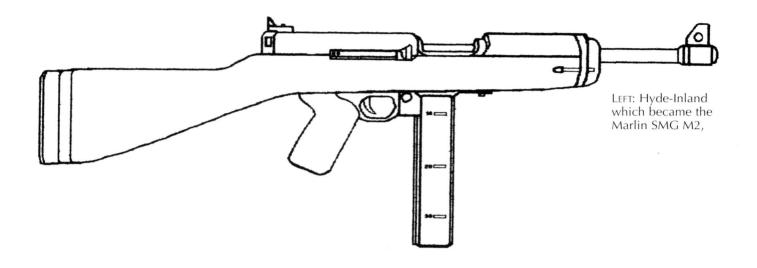

LEFT: Hyde-Inland which became the Marlin SMG M2,

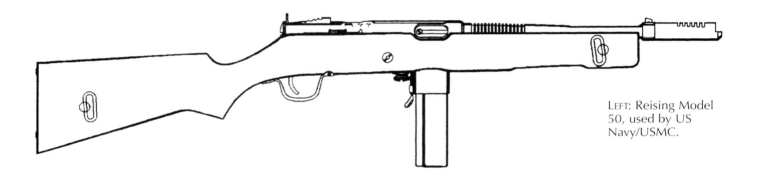

LEFT: Reising Model 50, used by US Navy/USMC.

Hyde-Inland/Marlin M2 Gun, Submachine, Calibre .45, M2

This was a further design by George Hyde that was made by the Inland Division of General Motors. It was a much improved Model 35, very neatly fashioned with handsome wood furniture, conventional blowback action, and lighter weight. This was tested by the US Army Ordnance Department in April 1942 and proved very promising. It had less recoil than the Thompson and little tendency to upward creep. It was also very accurate in close range and was better in auto fire than the Thompson though not so good in semi-auto. It passed mud and dust tests well. It had a rate of fire of 527 rpm. In over 6,000 test rounds there were 20 stoppages. Revisions were made by the designer, including alteration so that the gun would accept the then standard Thompson 30-round box magazine. With this gun there were only two stoppages in over 2,000 rounds of firing.

With minor improvements the gun was classed as Substitute Standard while provision was made for mass production as the new M2 SMG. As there was now a shortage of production facilities at existing arsenals, the contract went to the Marlin Firearms Co, New Haven, Connecticut. But setting up production proved difficult and manufacture did not start for another year—May 1943. By this time the much superior M3

ABOVE: Reising Model 50 being demonstrated by a US Navy sailor.

RIGHT: Thompson T2.

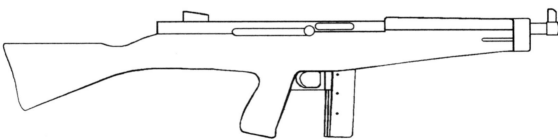

'Grease Gun' had been standardised, eliminating the need for the M2, so the contract was cancelled after about 400 guns had been made, though the initial contract of June 1942 was for 164,450 units.

Data:	M2
Calibre:	0.45in (11.43mm)
Length overall:	32.1in (815mm)
Length of barrel:	12.1in (307mm)
Weight:	9.25lb (4.2kg)
Muzzle velocity:	960ft/sec (293m/sec)
Rate of fire:	500rpm
Magazine capacity:	20 or 30 rounds
Fire options:	Automatic fire and single shot

Thompson T2 SMG

At the same time as the Hyde-Inland was submitted for trials to meet the new M2 SMG requirement, Auto-Ordnance also offered a new design for this requirement. Like the Hyde-Inland, there was extensive use of wood furniture and the usual simple blowback construction was used. There was a two-position trigger that controlled semi or full auto fire depending where the firer's finger was. prototypes were made with both .45in and 9mm calibre chambering. Tested against the Hyde-Inland, it proved inferior and was not selected for production.

Reising Model 50

This SMG was designed by Eugene C. Reising in the 1938-40 period. It was operated on the delayed blowback principle and had a rate of fire of 450-600 rpm. It had a 12 or 20-round magazine option, though the former was not produced for military service. It fired from a closed bolt which rose in a recess on top of the receiver. It was tested for military use on three occasions—August 1940, and July and November 1941, with improvements suggested each time. The gun was cocked by pulling back a rod through a slot under the front end of the wood furniture. The gun was never adopted by the US Army, but it was taken by the US Navy for issue to the Marines Corps. A later variant was the Model 55 in which the wood stock was replaced by a folding tubular stock and a pistol grip was fashioned behind the trigger. Some 10,000 units of both models were produced by Harrington and Richardson Arms Co in the 1941-45 period. While this gun performed well in ideal conditions, with few stoppages, it proved less successful in combat. Marines issued with the Reising for the Guadalcanal cam-

BELOW: The standard M3 SMG shows why it was nicknamed 'Grease Gun'. It is demonstrated by a US Army glider pilot in 1944. This was the mass-produced gun, largely of metal pressings, that replaced the Thompson SMG in production.

RIGHT: The M3 'Grease Gun' was swiftly in service with front line US troops. Here two infantrymen of the Third Army carry them during a refreshment break with local wine after capturing St Avold on 30 November 1944. Sling brackets (not swivels) were riveted on the left side of the receiver.

paign literally threw them away as useless since sand filled the recess on top of the gun and jammed the bolt.

Data:	Reising Model 50 (for USN/USMC)
Calibre:	0.45in (11.43mm)
Length:	35.75in (908mm)
Length of barrel:	11in (279mm)
Weight:	6.75 lb (3.06kg)
Muzzle velocity:	920ft/sec(280m/sec)
Rate of fire:	550rpm
Magazine capacity:	20 rounds
Fire options:	Automatic fire and single shot

United Defense UD-1

Because of the urgent need for guns to equip American allies, the United Defense Supply Corporation was formed in May 1941. It designed an ingenious SMG which combined both types of SMG chambering favoured by Allied nations, .45in calibre and 9mm, with a barrel to suit each calibre. The barrel not in use became the folding stock by screwing it to a fitting on the pistol grip. The box type 20-round magazine fitted on the left side and shells were ejected on the right. The prototype was tested by the US Army Ordnance Department in the latter part of 1942 and had a rate of fire of 1,150rpm and bad upward creep. It did not stand up to mud tests and was rejected.

United Defense M42

This was a more conventional design with a wooden stock and a vertical foregrip like the earlier Thompson SMGs. It was of conventional blowback type, firing with an open breech. Initial military tests in August 1940 found the rate of fire too high and the magazine inadequate. It was revised, in particular with a 40-round magazine made up of two 20-round boxes back-to-back which were turned when the first was empty. The modified model was tested against the Thompson T2 and the Hyde-Inland for the new M2 requirement. It was not adopted, however, but the 9mm version was demonstrated to the British and

Dutch Purchasing Commissions who ordered 15,000 between them, to be built by the Marlin Firearms Co. The Dutch guns were for use in the Dutch East Indies. The British guns were never issued to British forces but were all passed on to the Soviet Union in Lend-Lease aid.

Gun, Submachine, Calibre .45, M3

The success of the British Sten gun and the excellence of the German MP40 convinced the US Ordnance Department that a similar all-metal gun capable of simple production was needed for the US forces. It also had to be capable of conversion to fire .45in calibre or 9mm cartridges with minimal changes. Priority was given to this project in October 1942 and George Hyde was the designer, working with the Inland Division of GM. The Sten gun was studied for ideas, and design work was rapid with five prototypes, designated T15, ready for testing late in November 1942. With the single-shot facility removed for further simplification, the gun was redesignated T20. Extensive tests were carried out including 5,000 round firings with minimal stoppages recorded. One test for amphibious forces included dropping the gun in the surf and firing it immediately afterwards. The gun did the best of any tests in mud or dust. The magazine copied the MP40 design, no slings were provided, and most of the assembly was from simple metal stampings. Minor design problems were found but most could be easily corrected. The gun was standardised on 24 December 1942 as the M3 and provision was put in hand for mass production. This was to replace the SMG M1, M1A1 and M2 which were later reclassed as Limited Standard.

Production was ordered from the Guide Lamp Division of General Motors which in peacetime had been a specialist car lamp maker and had much experience of metal stamping production. An order for 300,000 M3s was given, production to start in May 1943 with production reaching 70,000 a month by September of that year. However, unexpected production difficulties and modifications to the gun reduced

BELOW LEFT: Chinese Peasant Militia men executing Nationalist landlords in 1950— possibly a posed propaganda picture. The two nearest men are using M1 type Thompsons which could be the real thing or Chinese copies. The third man appears to have a M3 'Grease Gun'.

COMPARISON

GUN, SUBMACHINE, CAL. .45
M3 AND M3A1

M3

M3A1

Modifications from M3 to M3A1

① LARGER EJECTION PORT
② RETRACTING HANDLE ELIMINATED
③ FINGER HOLE FOR COCKING
④ DISASSEMBLY GROOVES ADDED
⑤ STRONGER COVER SPRING
⑥ LARGER OIL CAN INSIDE GRIP
⑦ STOCK PLATE AND MAGAZINE FILLER
   ADDED TO STOCK
⑧ GUARD ADDED FOR MAGAZINE CATCH

M3

M3A1

ABOVE: Ordnance Department instructional sheet showing differences between SMGs M3 and M3A1.

the schedule and 32,000 a month was the best achieved, through 1944. Orders for 1944 exceeded 333,000, and the unit price was $18.36. The gun was designed for conversion to fire 9mm ammunition by changing the barrel, bolt and magazine feed, and in March 1944 there was an urgent order for 25,000 guns so converted. These were parachuted to resistance groups in Europe for the invasion of NW Europe. Total production by the end of the war in 1945 was 606,694 units. A silencer and flash hider were produced for the gun for use in clandestine operations and night landings, etc.

The somewhat unmilitary appearance of this functional SMG led to its famous nick-name of 'Grease Gun' which is what it closely resembled.

Gun, Submachine, Calibre .45, M3A1

Service experience with the M3 showed up a few failings. In addition its manufacture was studied to see where further simplification and modifications could be made. The bolt handle tended to break off, so on the improved version it was eliminated altogether and the gun was cocked instead by putting a finger into a hole in the bolt and pulling it back. All the working parts were altered where necessary to make it easier to dis-assemble the weapon for cleaning and repair, the safety lever was moved, and a bracket was added on the rear of the stock to help hand-loading the magazines, and to act as a stop for the cleaning rod. The barrel collar had flats cut into so that the stock could be used as a wrench to unscrew the barrel assembly. The rearsight was strengthened, and the modified sight and stock were also featured in later production M3s. The prototype of the modified M3 was designated M3E1 and in December 1944 the design was officially accepted by the Ordnance Dept and was standardised as the M3A1. It replaced the M3 in production and 15,469 were built during 1945 before the war ended.

Data:	M3 and M3A1
Calibre:	0.45in (11.43mm)
Length overall:	29.8in (757mm)
Length with stock folded:	
	22.8in (579mm)
Weight:	8.15lb (3.7kg)
Muzzle velocity:	920ft/sec
	(280m/sec)
Rate of fire:	350-450 rpm
Magazine capacity:	30 rounds
Fire options:	Automatic fire only

Thompson SMG M1928A1 and M1, Chinese copies

In 1940 China was one of the nations buying Thompson SMGs from Auto-Ordnance and after the Lend-Lease Act of 1941 thousands more were supplied. The guns supplied were originally M1928A1, then M1s. To obtain more guns, and repair the US-supplied ones some ordnance factories in China were copying the guns and making their own even before the war ended. When the Communist faction drove out the Nationalist faction in 1949 they continued to manufacture replica Thompson SMGs. Apart from the Chinese inscriptions they resembled the American models though quality was variable. The guns were supplied to Communist Chinese allies including the North Koreans and the Viet Cong and were used against American troops in both the Korean and Vietnam conflicts.

In 1951 the Munich Arms Corporation acquired the assets, tools, and spares of the Auto-Ordnance Corporation. By that time production of the Thompson SMG had long ago ceased (at the end of 1944) though spares were still supplied. In the 1980s the Munich Arms Corporation did make a limited run of Model 1928 guns with minor changes, mainly to supply the needs of the film, TV, and theatrical industries, though some may have gone to private individuals.

End of an era—nearly!

In April 1945 all Thompson SMGs of Models M1928A1, M1 and M1A1 in US Army service were declared obsolete and were ordered to be withdrawn and replaced by the new M3 and M3A1 'Grease Gun'. This officially saw the end of the Tommy Gun in United States' military service, but many of the withdrawn weapons were reconditioned and supplied post-war to United States Allies, mainly small nations, where they saw further service. However, US Navy personnel of the inshore patrols were still using Thompson M1s in the Vietnam war, over 20 years later. Some ex-service guns were purchased privately and many found their way to terrorist organisations or other illicit users. Despite being a design over 80 years old in concept, it is likely that even today a few are still in the inventory of political insurrectionists and not entirely displaced by Kalashnikovs and other modern types.

Anatomy of the Tommy Gun

BELOW: Cross-section through the Model 1923 Military Thompson, from Thompson brochure.

BOTTOM: Viet Cong or Chinese copy of Thompson M1 with no butt and with the early form of L-shaped simplified 'peep' backsight.

The Thompson SMG, in all models, was a well-engineered weapon designed as a quality product and built to a high standard. This was reflected in its reliability and robustness. Though it changed in details through the different production models, the essential elements of construction remained the same. To show all the parts in minute details require a complex instruction manual which the Auto-Ordnance company produced. In fact it produced a wealth of literature on all aspects of the gun, and the US Army also produced TMs on the different models it used. There is not space here to cover every minute detail, but some useful diagrams are reproduced. The cross-section shows the M1928A1 and comes from the US Army TM on the weapon. The larger diagram is from an Auto-Ordnance brochure and shows the main groups and components that make up the M1921 model. The final cross-section shows the Model 1923 Military model and is useful in showing the spring feed arrangement in the box magazine which pushes the rounds up into the chamber.

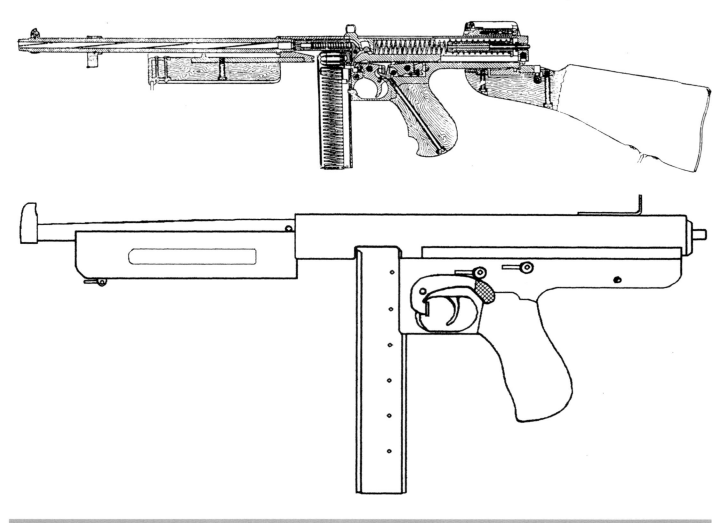

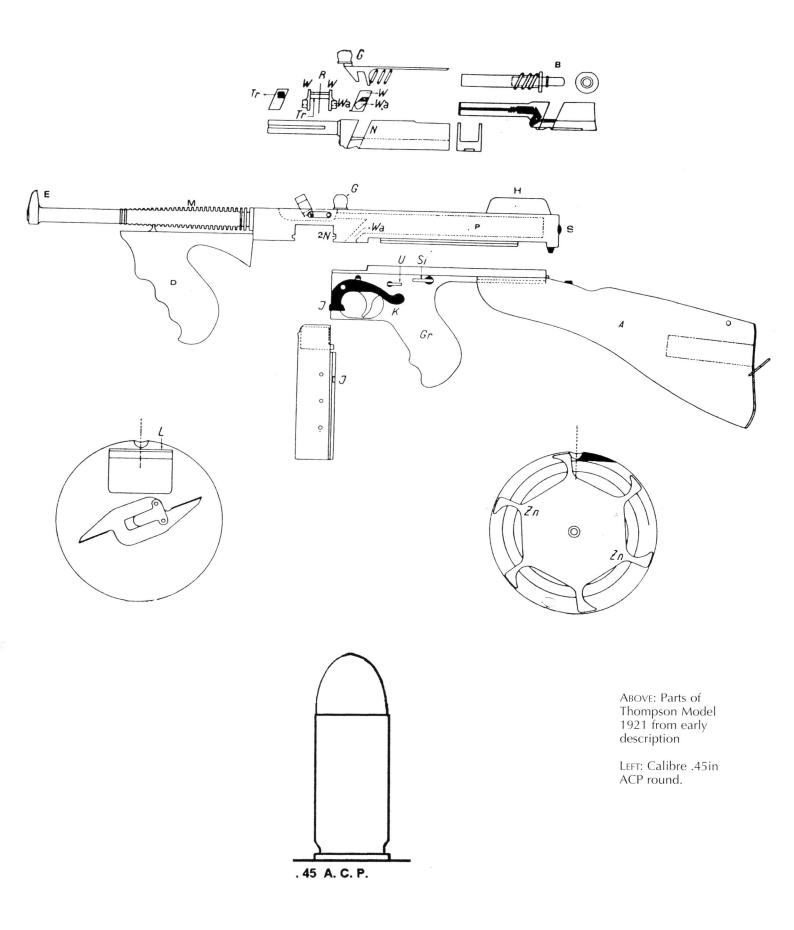

.45 A.C.P.

ABOVE: Parts of Thompson Model 1921 from early description

LEFT: Calibre .45in ACP round.

Anatomy

The groups break down into barrel and receiver, frame, bolts and spring, and magazine.

Dimensions of parts (Model 1928)

Overall length, stock omitted:
    23.2in (59cm)
Overall length, with stock:
    31.8in (80.7cm)
Barrel length: 10.5in (26.3cm)
Bore length: 9.76in (24.4cm)
Rifling: One turn, RH, in
    16in (40cm)
Distance, heel of butt behind receiver:
    8.6in (21.5cm)
Distance, heel of butt below receiver:
    3.3in (8.2cm)

Weights of components

Complete gun less magazine and butt:
    8.5lb (3.8kg)
Butt: 1.5lb (0.68kg)
50-round drum magazine, Type L:
    2.5lb (1.14kg)

Blowback cycle and operation

(Gun firing from an open bolt)

1. Loaded magazine is inserted.

2. Bolt drawn to the rear, compressing the main spring. Sear holds bolt in the open position.

3. Press trigger. This causes sear to release the bolt. Bolt is driven forward by the coiled recoil spring and first cartridge is pushed into bolt path by the magazine spring.

4. Firing pin strikes the primer and the extractor catches the cartridge rim.

5. Cartridge fires, and pressure forces the bullet forward and case to rear. Initial velocity of bolt is low and bullet exits barrel before bolt opens.

6. Bolt travels to rear under the pressure of the explosion, taking empty cartridge case with it. Case hits ejector and is forced out through ejector port. Bolt travelling to rear compresses the spring again.

7. Compressed spring stops rearward movement of bolt which impacts on the receiver. This drives the bolt forward again and the same cycle repeats as the next round is forced into the path of the bolt.

Stoppages

Stoppages could be caused by a feed jam, failure of magazine to feed in round, or a defective cartridge. A faulty extractor could also fail to eject an empty case, jamming the next round into the chamber. Drill for the latter was to remove the magazine, draw the bolt right back, and allow the live round to slide out of the receiver; the unejected case was then pulled or prodded out. For a misfire the bolt was also drawn quickly to the rear to eject the misfired round. If the magazine failed to feed it was removed, the top round was taken out in case it was wrongly positioned, and the magazine was put back into the firing position. If it still failed to feed it was removed and replaced by a new magazine. Dented or damaged magazines could give rise to failure to feed.